Sally and the daisy

Story by Beverley Randell
Illustrated by Meredith Thomas

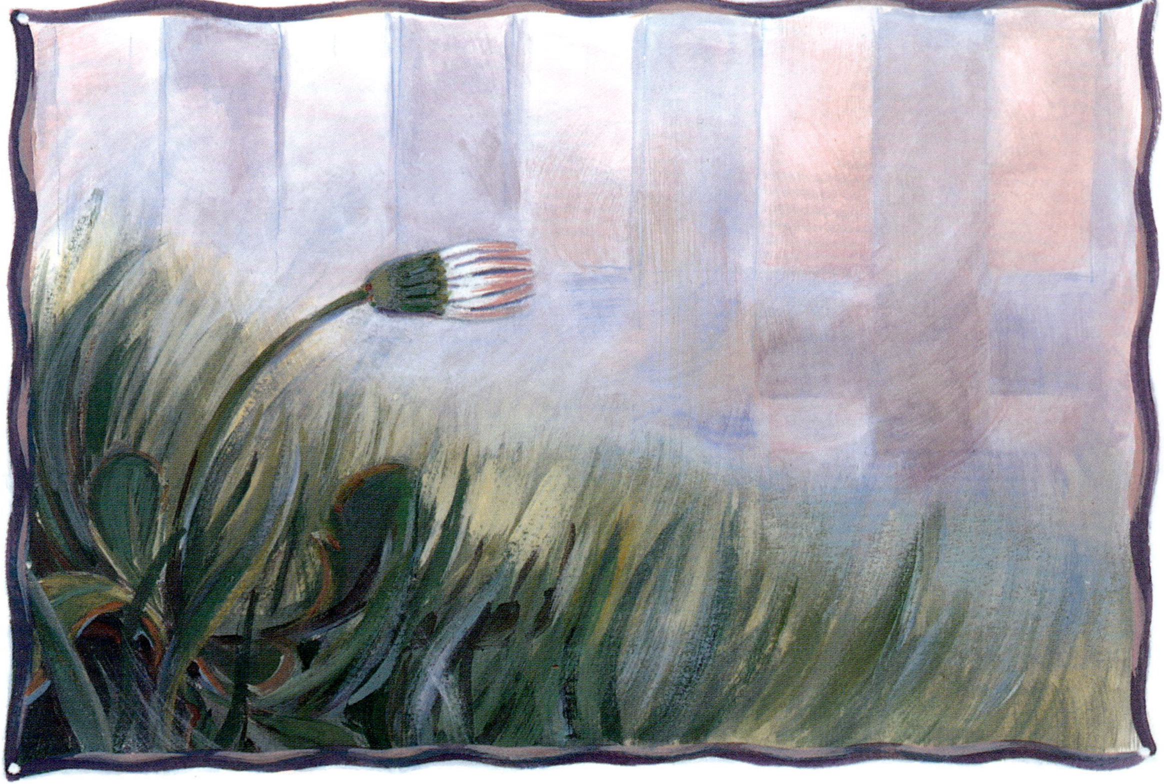

The daisy is asleep.

4

Here comes Sally.
Can Sally see the daisy?
No.
The daisy is asleep.

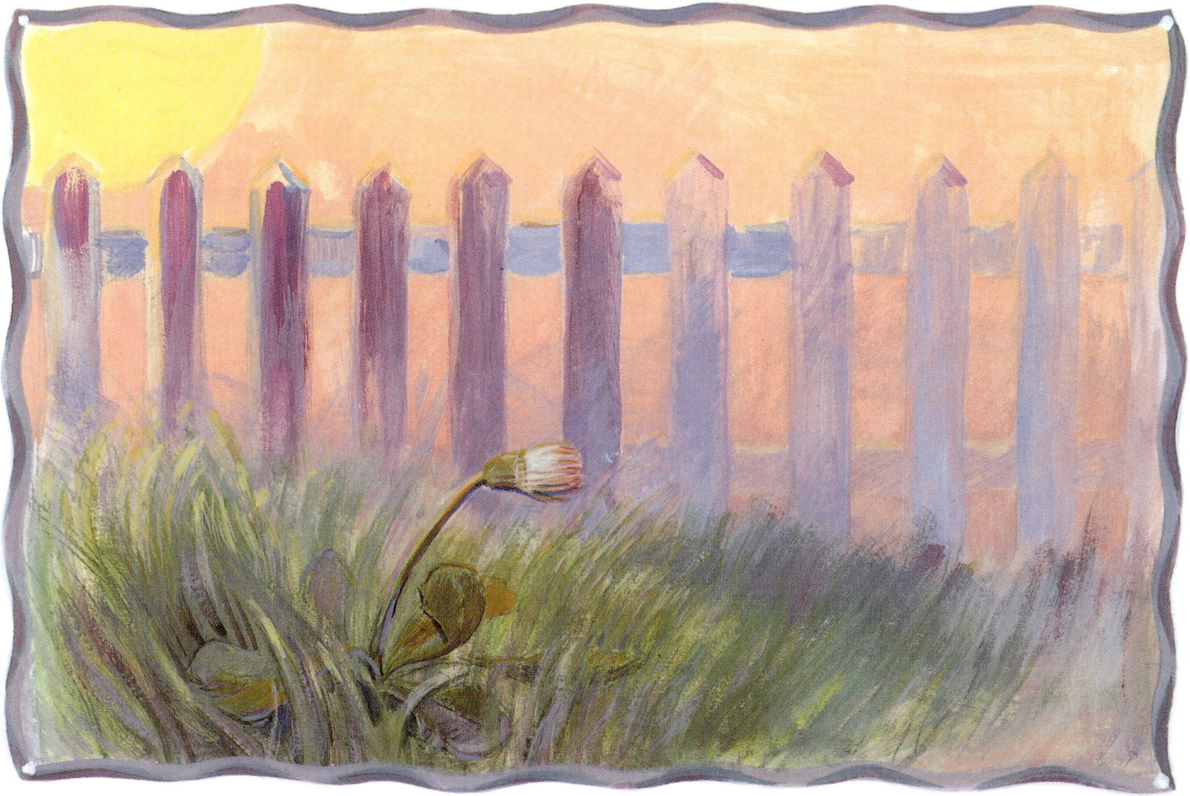

Here comes the sun.
Wake up, daisy.

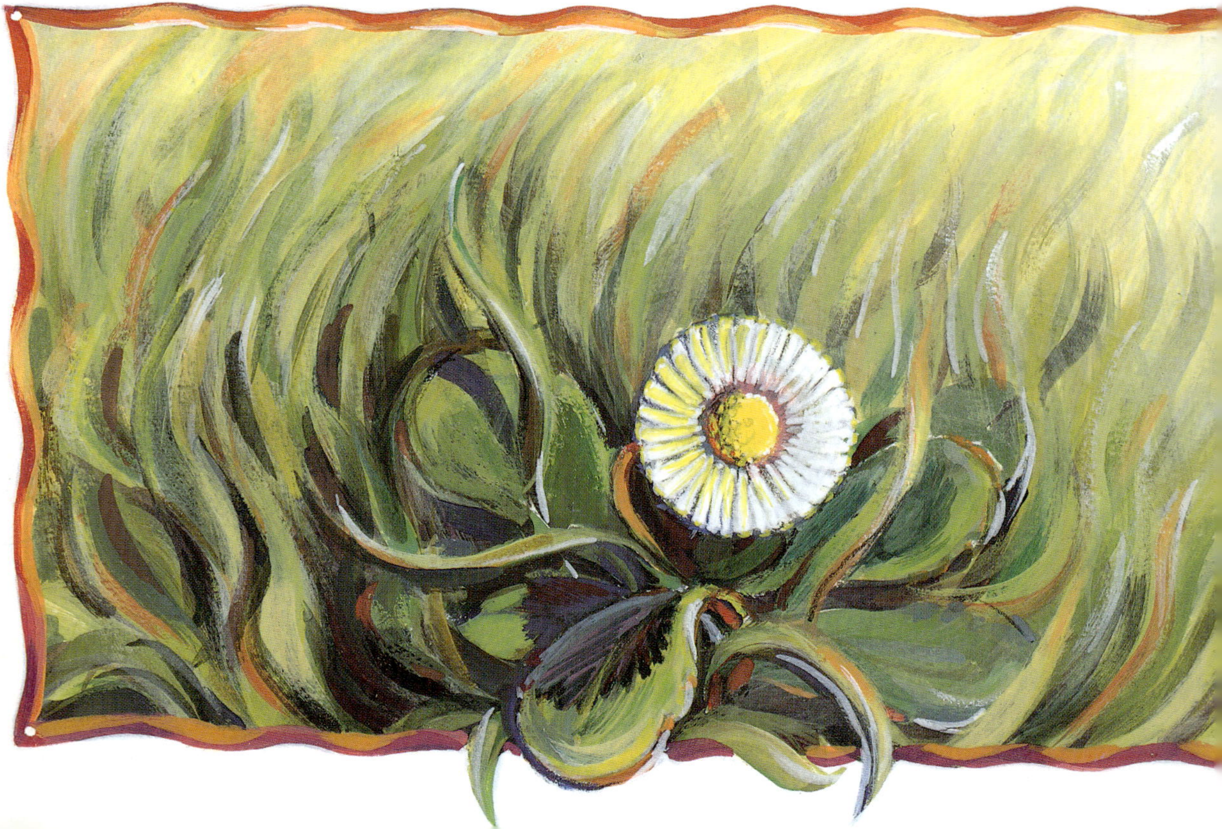

The sun is on the daisy.
The daisy wakes up.

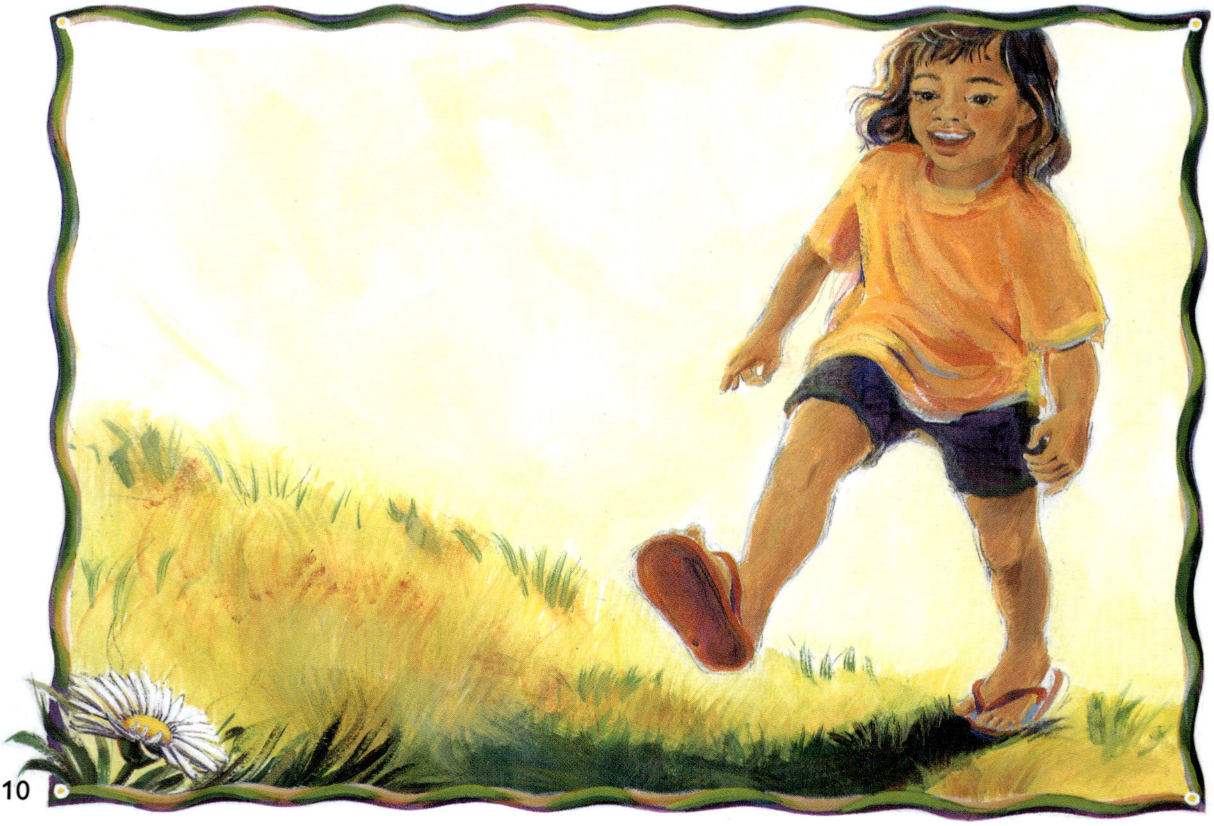

Here comes Sally.
Sally can see the daisy.

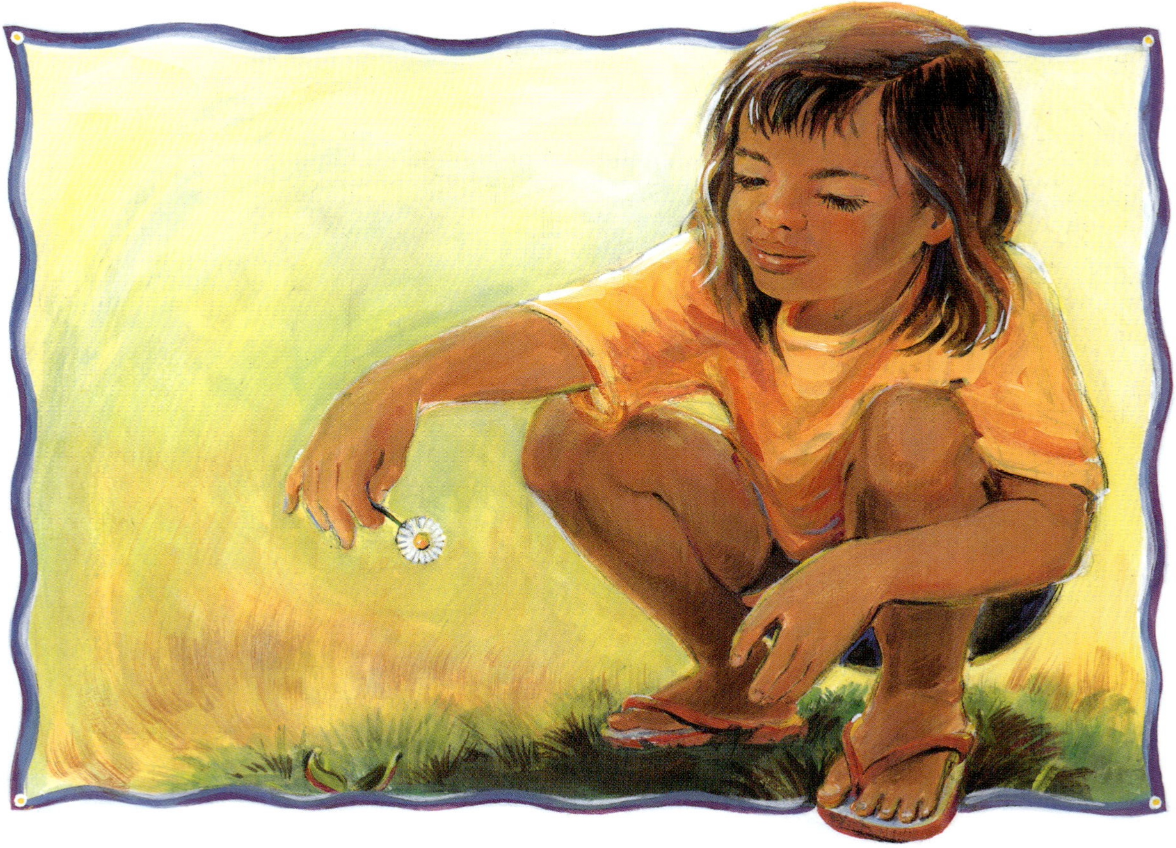

"Look!
A daisy!
Here is a daisy."

"Mum, Mum!
Here is a daisy for you."

"Thank you, Sally."